A Simply Classic

Nutcracker

For Elementary to Late Elementary Pianists

Peter Ilyich Tchaikovsky / Arranged by Margaret Goldston

This collection features excerpts from *The Nutcracker Suite,* simplified for first- or second-year piano students. *The Nutcracker* is an orchestral ballet written in 1891 by the famous Russian composer, Peter Ilyich Tchaikovsky (1840-1893). The eight selections included in this collection are the same as those chosen by Tchaikovsky for the orchestral suite.

Listen to the orchestral recordings of *The Nutcracker Suite* and have fun capturing the excitement of Tchaikovsky's music in your performance! Imagine that you are performing with an orchestra as you combine the solos with the teacher duets for an impressive recital. The magic of *The Nutcracker* can be yours with these arrangements.

For more simplified arrangements of favorite classical pieces, you may be interested in some of my other collections:

> A *Simply Classic Christmas* (#17384)
> *Simply Classic, Book 1* (#6052)
> *Simply Classic, Book 2* (#14706)

Enjoy!

Alfred

The Story of the
Nutcracker

This is a magical tale about a young girl, Clara, and her most exciting Christmas ever! While her parents prepare for a Christmas party, the Christmas tree is being decorated with colorful, sparkling lights. Clara and her brother, Fritz, invite their friends to play and dance with them.

Clara's godfather, Herr Drosselmeyer, a strange and mysterious man, presents Clara and Fritz with gifts. Clara's gift, a beautiful Nutcracker, is the hit of the party. A little jealous, Fritz grabs the Nutcracker from Clara and breaks it. Clara sadly puts the Nutcracker doll to sleep in a toy bed before going to bed herself. After the guests depart and the family is asleep, a heartbroken Clara sneaks back downstairs to see her beloved Nutcracker.

Suddenly, strange things begin to happen! The tree grows to an enormous height. The room fills with an army of mice, led by the Mouse King. The Nutcracker comes to life and leads a group of toy soldiers to battle. Just as it seems that the soldiers are about to lose the fight, Clara throws her slipper at the Mouse King and all of the mice flee.

The Nutcracker turns into a handsome prince and invites Clara to come with him to a land of snow and enchanted forests. She is welcomed by dancing Snowflakes before moving on to the Kingdom of Sweets. There they are met by the Sugarplum Fairy, who leads them into the palace for a celebration of dances (Russian Dance, Arabian Dance, Chinese Dance and Dance of the Reed Flutes). Beautiful waltzing flowers are joined by all of the ballet dancers for the last dance.

Miniature Overture

*Played before the ballet begins, the overture is followed
by the curtain rising on "The Party Scene"*

Peter Ilyich Tchaikovsky
Arr. by Margaret Goldston

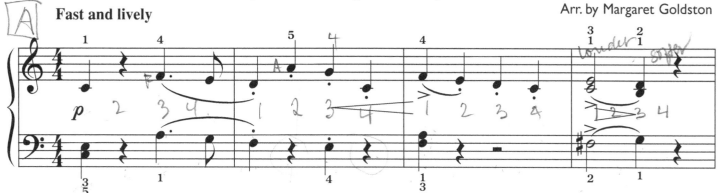

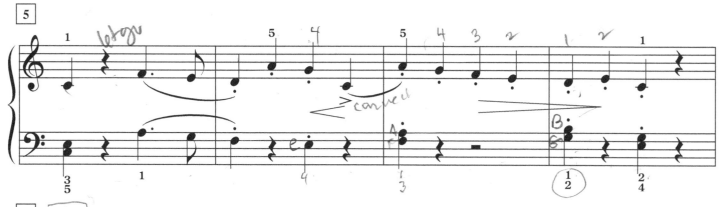

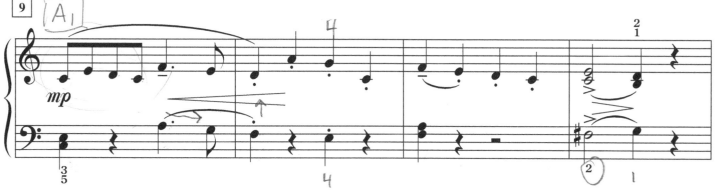

DUET PART (Student plays 1 octave higher than written.)

Fast and lively

4

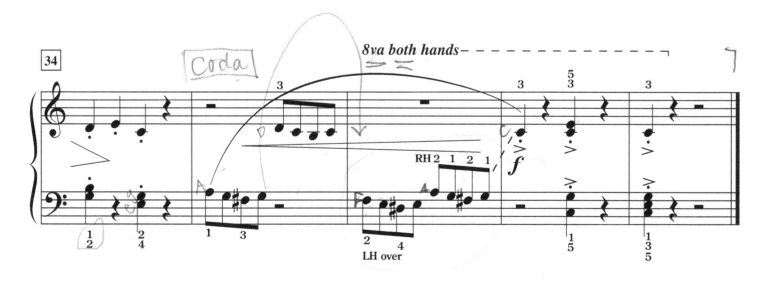

March

Clara, Fritz, and their playmates have a parade.
They put on paper hats and march around the room.

Peter Ilyich Tchaikovsky
Arr. by Margaret Goldston

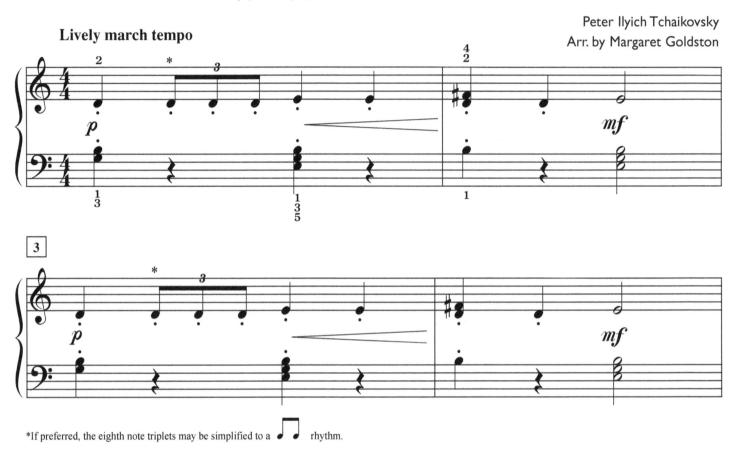

*If preferred, the eighth note triplets may be simplified to a ♩♪ rhythm.

DUET PART (Student plays 1 octave higher than written.)

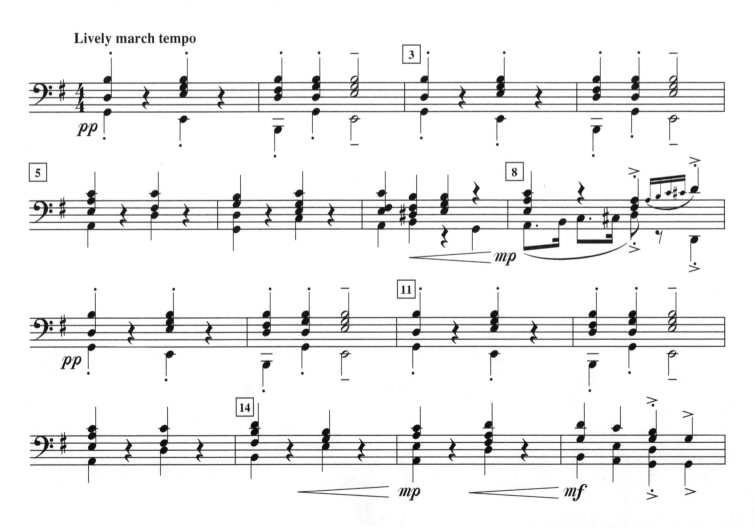

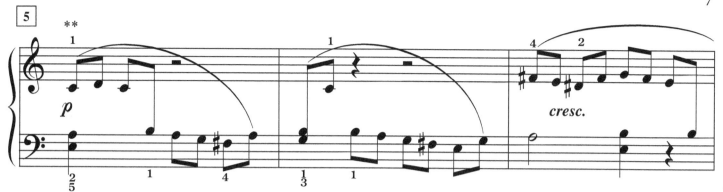

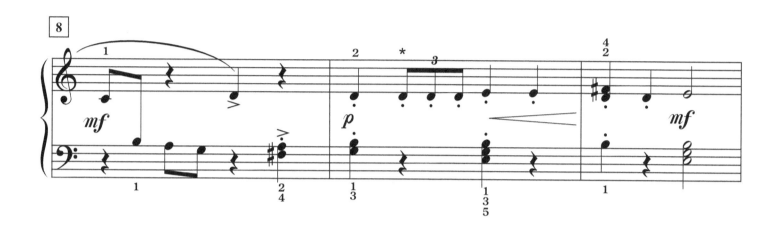

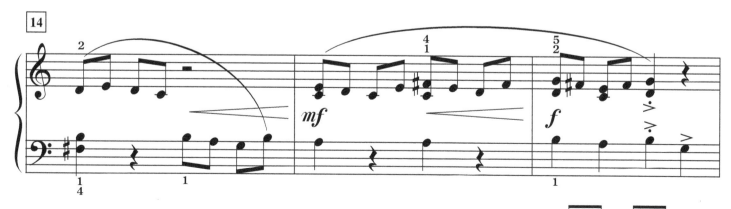

**The eighth notes in measures 5–8, 13–16 and 29–32 may be played unevenly, in a "lilting" style:

long   short   long   short, *etc.*

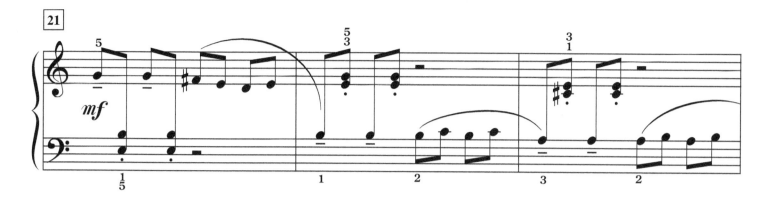

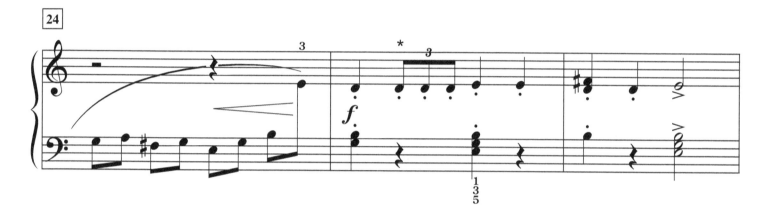

Dance of the Sugarplum Fairy

The Sugarplum Fairy dances a solo for Clara and the Nutcracker Prince.

Peter Ilyich Tchaikovsky
Arr. by Margaret Goldston

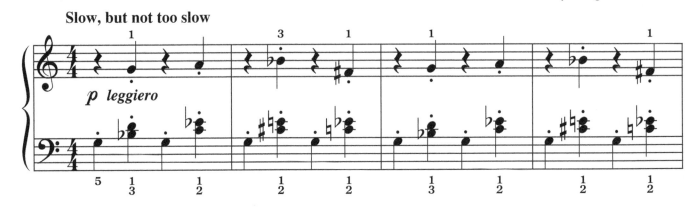

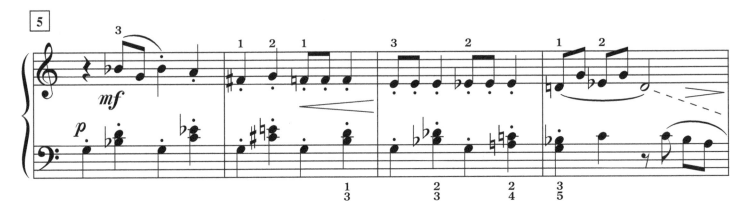

DUET PART (Student plays 1 octave higher than written.)

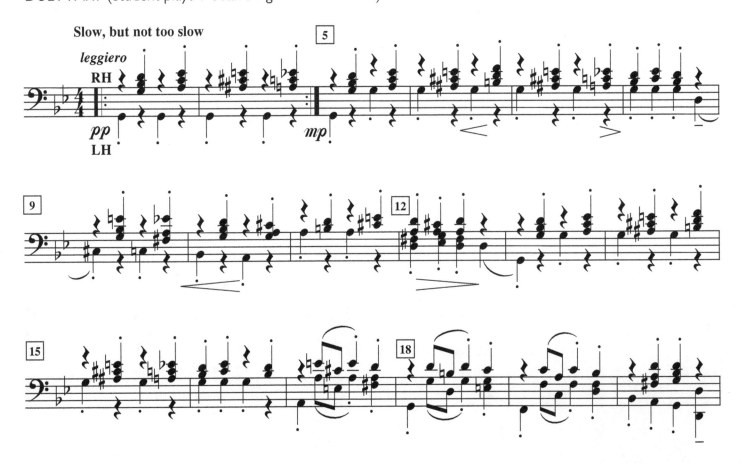

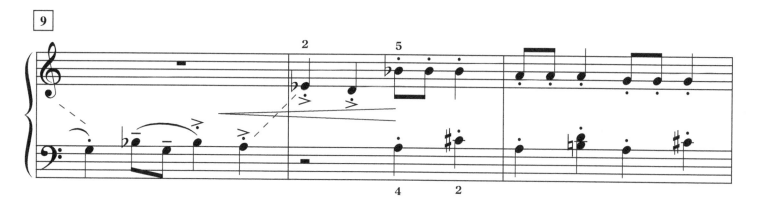

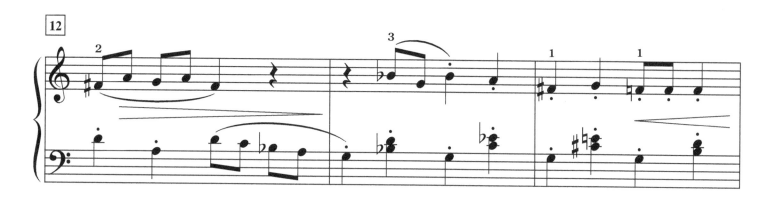

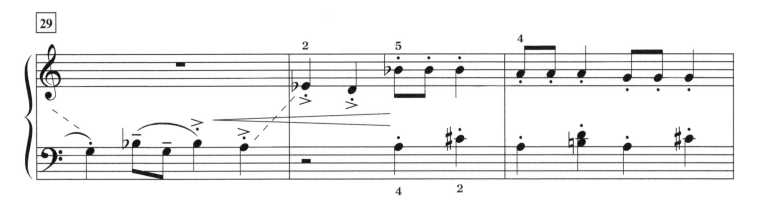

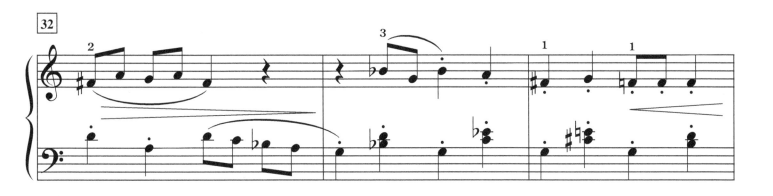

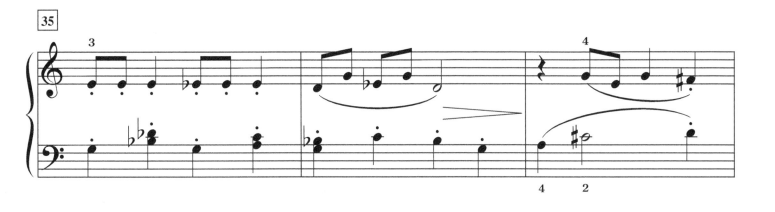

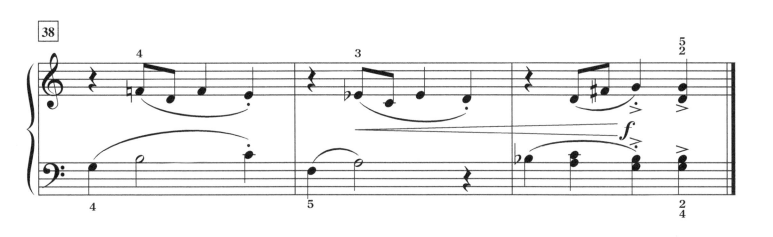

Russian Dance

This is the first of the banquet dances from around the world.

Peter Ilyich Tchaikovsky
Arr. by Margaret Goldston

Very lively

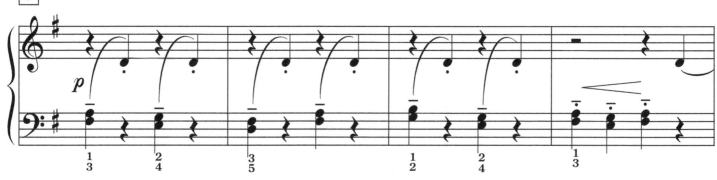

DUET PART (Student plays 1 octave higher than written.)

Very lively

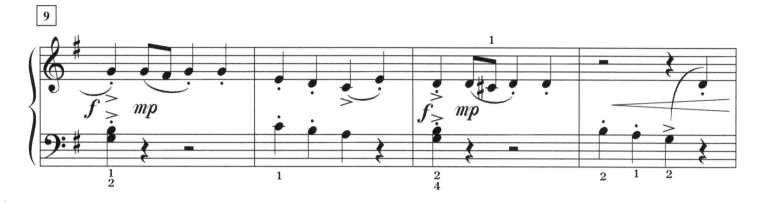

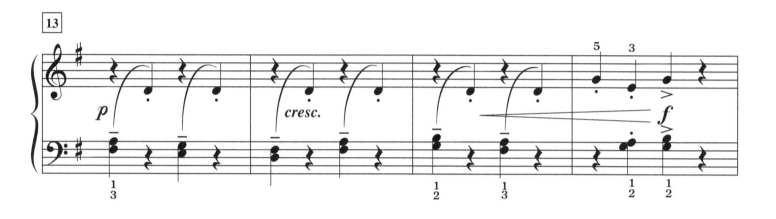

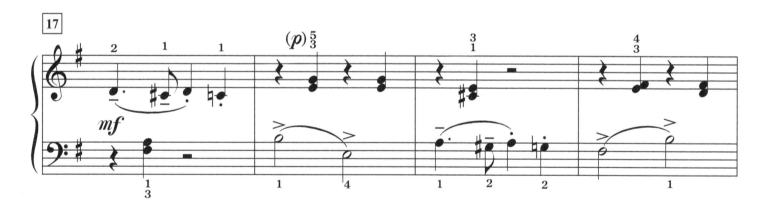

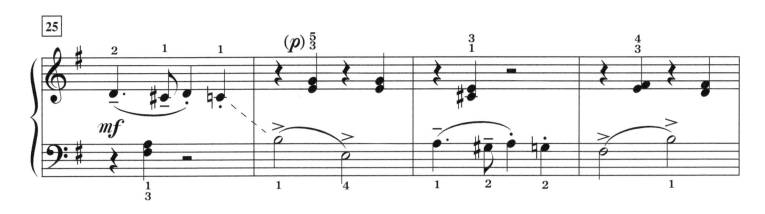

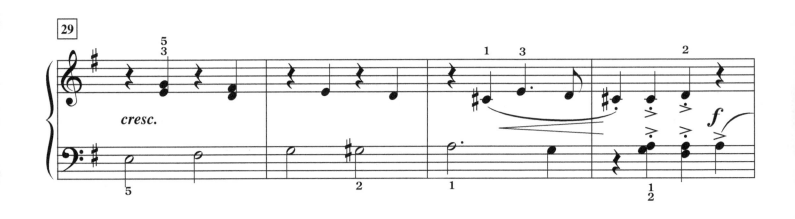

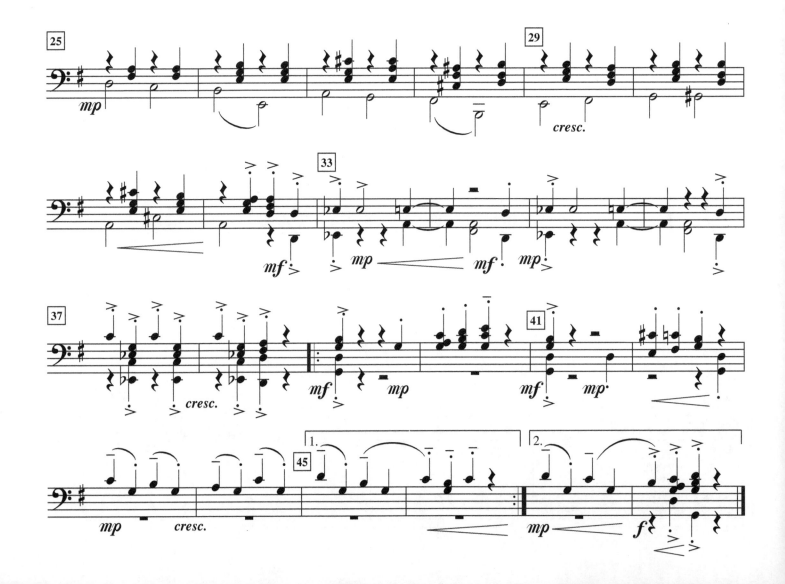

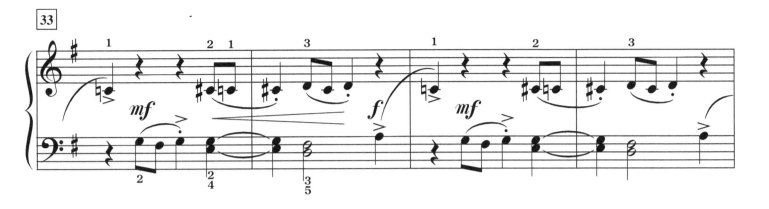

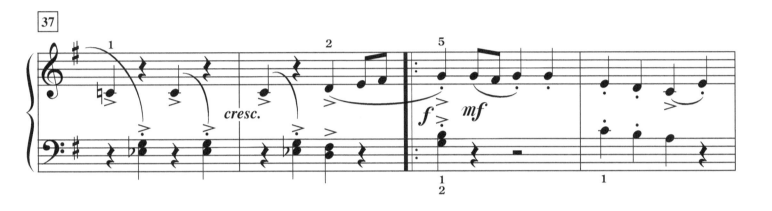

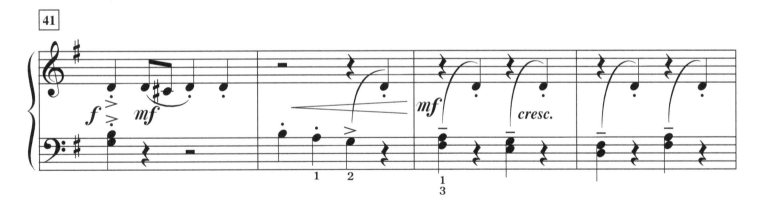

Arabian Dance

Peter Ilyich Tchaikovsky
Arr. by Margaret Goldston

DUET PART (Student plays 1 octave higher than written.)

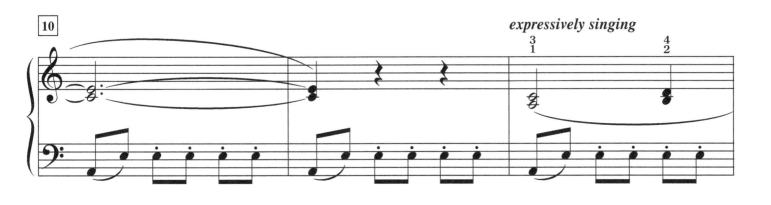

expressively singing

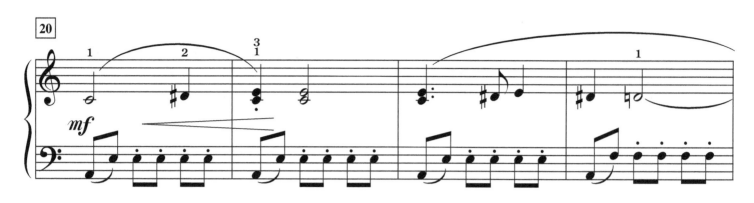

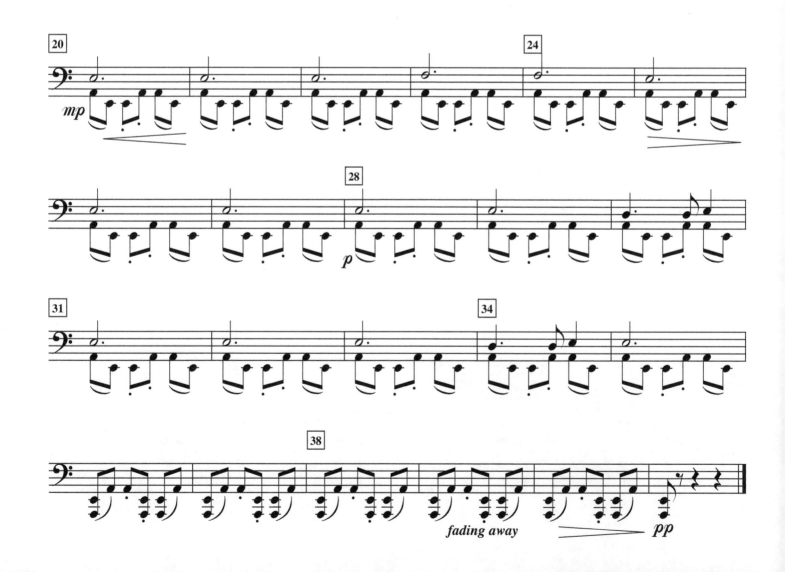

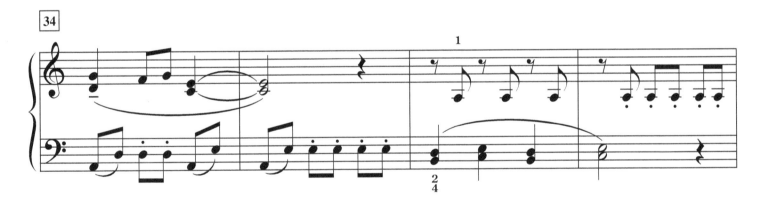

Chinese Dance

Peter Ilyich Tchaikovsky
Arr. by Margaret Goldston

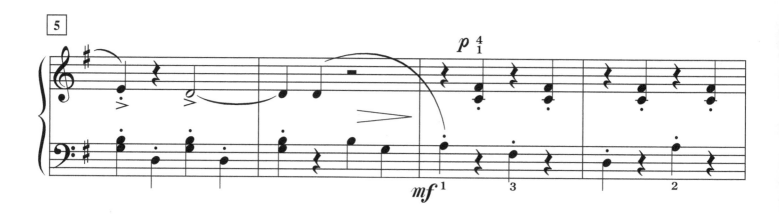

DUET PART (Student plays 1 octave higher than written.)

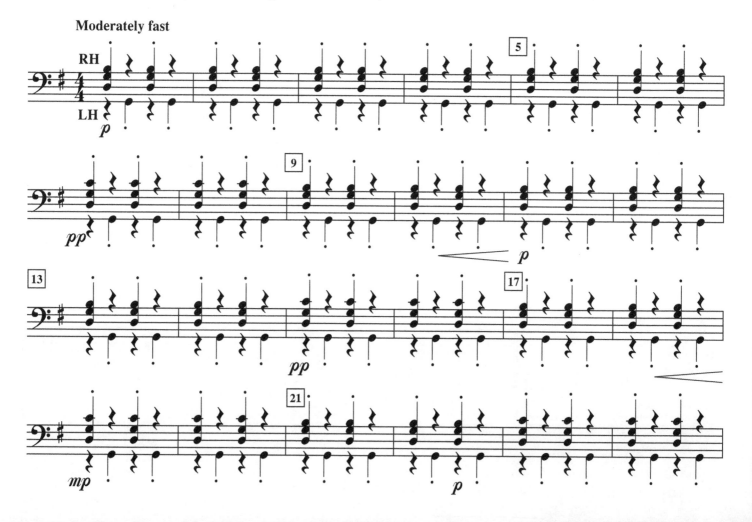

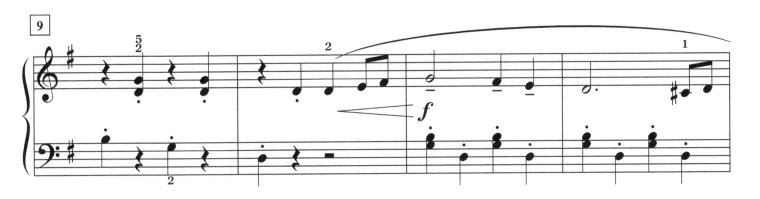

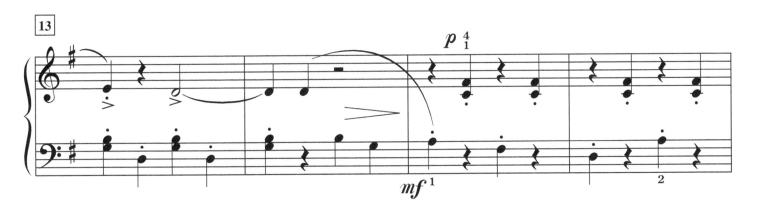

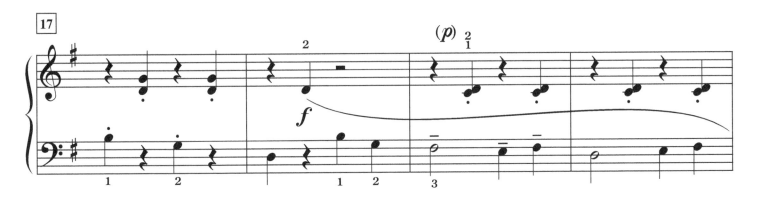

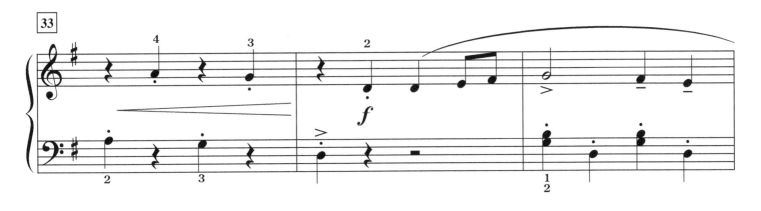

Dance of the Reed Flutes

Peter Ilyich Tchaikovsky
Arr. by Margaret Goldston

DUET PART (Student plays 1 octave higher than written.)

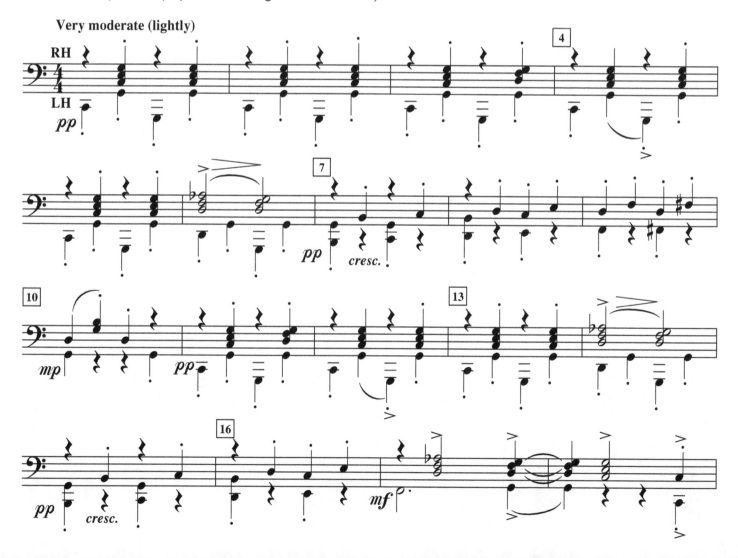

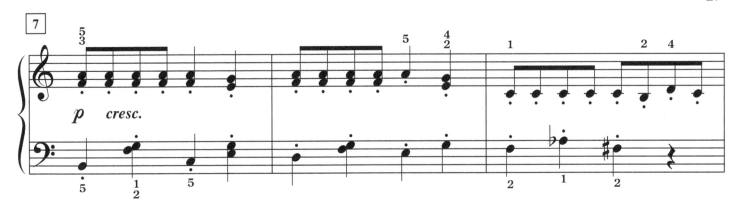

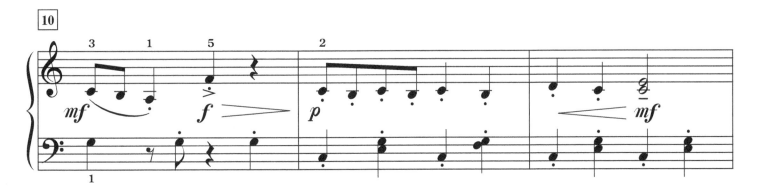

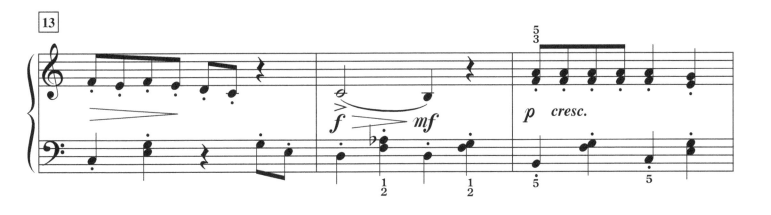

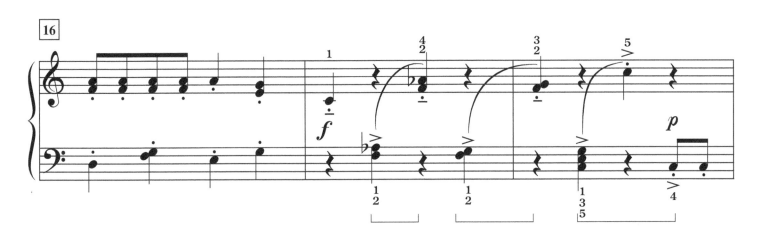

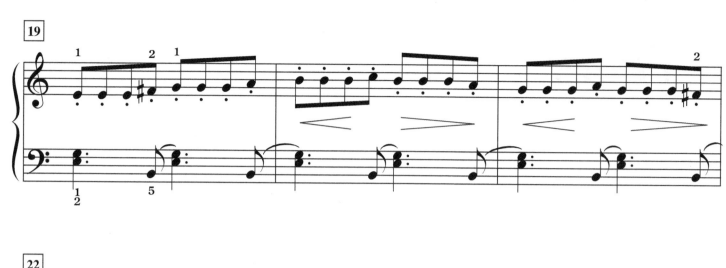

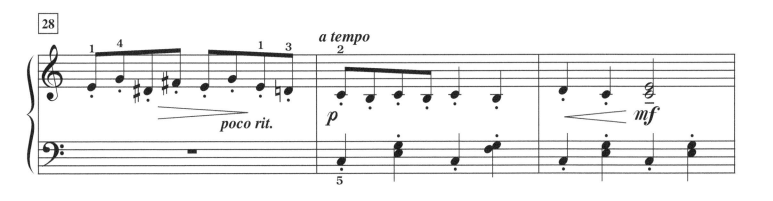

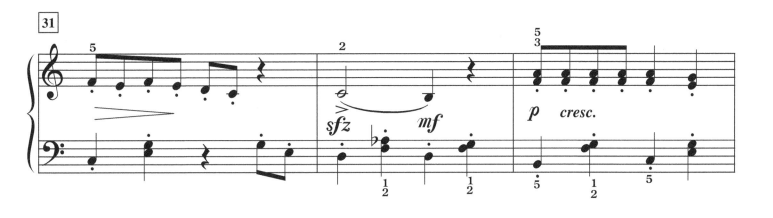

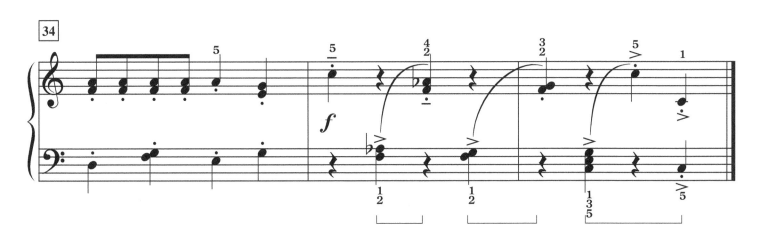

Waltz of the Flowers

Peter Ilyich Tchaikovsky
Arr. by Margaret Goldston

DUET PART (Student plays 1 octave higher than written.)

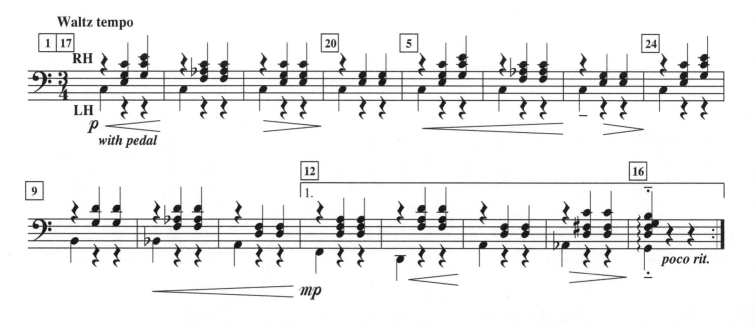

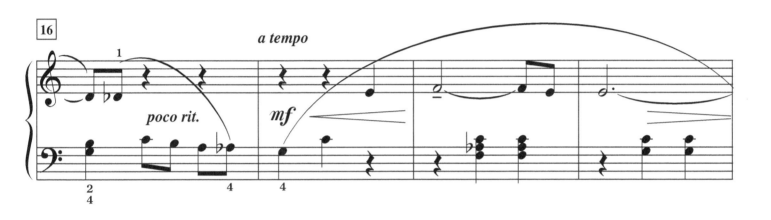

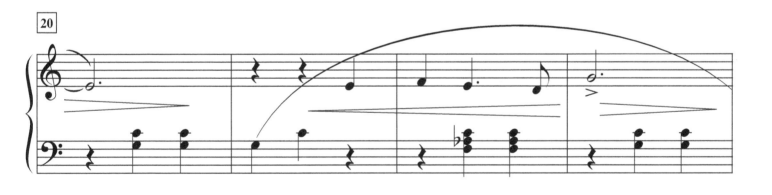

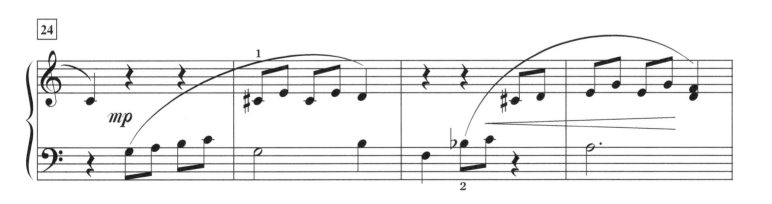

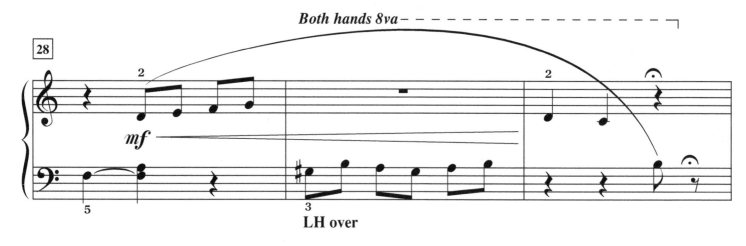

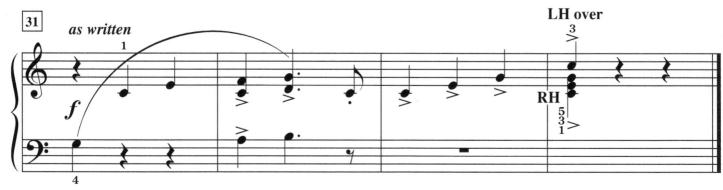

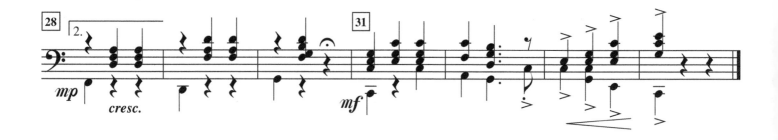

*Clara and the Nutcracker Prince reigned happily forever over that
magical kingdom, where there are still as many wonders as ever…
at least for those who have eyes to discover them.*